cran

cran
American Fruit Poems

eran eads

REBEL SATORI PRESS

New Orleans & New York

Published in the United States of America by
Rebel Satori Press
www.rebelsatoripress.com

Cover Art: Juan Davila, Fig. 300, 2021, Acrylic on paper 105 x 75cm, © Juan Davila, Courtesy Kalli Rolfe Contemporary Art; Photography: Mark Ashkanasy

Paperback ISBN: 978-1-60864-284-7

Library of Congress Control Number: 2023944418

for Jesus

Contents

It hasn't been an easy 100 years

First there was the war
ble. Then the steady song of worry
for what might be the rest of a life.
You could enlist the help of others,
join a collective, and begin prosper
procedures or dream of your farm!
Doing both is about as exhausting
as family. And, we use them too.
If you want your farm to be useful
you must first have a farm. Family
is the same way. Workers can be
made to work. It has been found
Cranberry workers in Oregon
were once *paid per peck*. Really,
it hasn't been an easy 100 years.
Google the year *the President
ate applesauce*. The year we saw
something hideous and thought
harvest. A bog became a way to
grow berries. The year of tractors!
Water became a method of frost
resistance.

To a man with a farm

The world was a field.
Sometimes, I said *be the farmer*
and he knew what to do. He built
me a bed. He slept with me. He woke
when the sun rose and left for work.
I measured my *adaptability indices*
and found surprising and favorable
results. I forgot about science on days
he kissed me. Wandered eager at night.
I think it was the up-keep.
Perhaps the long days, the shorter
nights, the exhaustion of creating
and having to care for something
that continued to eagerly change.
I wanted to be on his farm. I wanted
to be farmed.   To fruit.
But it is always the up-keep.
All I am is best when farmed.
And all he saw of me was field.

"Understanding Cranberry Frost and Winter Hardiness"[1]

When I saw you, I wanted to test
my cold-hardiness levels, wanted
to be cooled and freeze-resistant.
I became my own mechanism,
a temperature-tolerant, close-
branching thing. Dense. Capable
of surrounding myself for warmth.
I wanted to ripen by your arrival:
cranberry & frost. To be softened
by your cold. Be a significant study
of your useful ruthless nature on things
that fruit. But it got more cold.
I worried I would begin to be
sensitive, freeze from within.
Like any good bushberry, I bounced
back to let ice propagate *through
the calyx end of the fruit.* I gave
myself *chilling hours* and measured
my effectiveness at surviving you.
I repeated *this set of experiments.*
I confirmed the data.

1   Title is taken from an article of the same name written by Beth
Ann A. Workmaster and Jiwan P. Palta in Department of Horticulture
University of Wisconsin, Madison, WI 53706

cran

Named after the head
of a crane; sure there
is the color and maybe
a rudeness to be round,
willingness. An ability
to appear in a bog.
There are individuals
that group. Groups clump
during reaping. Heaps
are moved together with
tactics of dispersal.
Loosed from shrubs,
collected up using wet-
-harvesting methods
invented by berry enthusiasts
looking to glean more
productively. When I want
a name, and I often do,
I can never find it. Sometimes
fruit. Sometimes vine.

Have you ever been a weapon
used against yourself to cause
growth? Okay,
in the language
of agriculture: a powerful tool
producing what would otherwise
require many other human-hands
to till the earth of? Perhaps
even involving farming animals
and their ability to haul, perhaps
once you were made and became
useful, a farmer was freed to focus
on other crops.

History with Red Pole-Barn Freezer & Berries

The goats ate the branches;
the geese, the leaves,
and the berries were boiled
down into jams or mixed
with other sweeter rosehips
made ripe by the cold. Or
they were kept for winter
in wood boxes surrounded
by water. Every December
morning could involve fruit
even when the snow made
it difficult to go into town,
cranberries were a possibility
with milk and breakfast oats.
Some were frozen with
the blueberries and green peas.
And we ate them as a treat.
As we scraped the year-
long-frozen-salmon from
its labeled butcher paper,
we snuck mouthfuls, mixing
for taste, always hoping for
an extra raspberry bag to be
left unattended by those who
guarded the frozenness and left

them high and hard to reach.
Springtime boys were workers:
we watched new buds extend
on the highbush, as the slow
tractor made its way to the barn.
There was the summer of cranberry
honey and it was the kind of bitter
I remember. Mostly we let the bees
decide and they chose fireweed
and clover. There were days
when it all was so ordinary. Then
the fall would whisk in some cold
and it would all smell of sweet new rot,
four-leafs everywhere on that island,
cranberries ripening, & ready for the year.

[When I discovered]

When I discovered
the sun, I discovered
a yellow ball.
And I drew it.
The sun was small,
round as a berry,
and sitting in the
upper right hand
side of each page.
Then, it grew out.
Lines came down,
only a few of them
but they were sharp
and purposeful.
Then the ball fell
down a bit and was
surrounded by lines
until it disappeared
too and was replaced
with only vertical
lines repeated until
the page could not
be seen.

[Then I discovered]

I had not really
discovered the sun
nor even a new way
to look at it, nor even
a new way to put
it down
for memory.
The first letters I wrote
were *J, K, & L* repeated
over and over and over.
I held the notebook up
and asked my father
what the word was.
Most times, it was *nothing*
then sometimes, he said
it's close to juke
kill, luck, jult.
Then vowels came
and more letters
and more sounds.
[dash] Sun sat
upper right corner
by the only paper
color left on the paper.
The sky was filling
the rest of the page.

I knew I could not
make new discoveries.
But I stumbled over
my scribbles until
I could finally scrawl
joke!

When Someone Shouts Pansy On South Pickett Lane

what he means is the cold won't kill you.
He means he can see that you bloom,
means your petals are a mouth and he
considered it.　　　　The snow is so
delicate with you. Like nothing is delicate.

Snowberry

May not be beautiful
and may not be well
behaved

but interesting throughout
the year: from bell shaped
blooms past berrying fall.

Naturally found
in swampy thickets
but able to thrive in the dry.

Their showiest feature lasts into winter.

Greenhouse

Even in an artificial day
it was easy to grow.
Nutrient-rich water helped.
Warmth and light, too.
Only when he said
this is a walkway, was it
the way to walk; repetitive
stepping made the ground
hard, boot-ready.
How are the berries rooting
was only asked if blemish
was discovered on leaves.
Until then, the stems were
clearly alive and growing
experimentally high. Each
day there was progress,
each stem would lean a bit
and then push itself up.
This miraculous performance
lasted a full summer season.
There was a way to grow real
fruit in this fake weather,
this fourteen hour light.
I think I could have stayed
alive.

"No One Grower Can Do It Alone"

It takes a village to raise
a successful cranberry
farm. And here, here it is.
Marketing experts are here
to do what marketing experts do.
Let's consider craisins!
Have you pondered
the extension of seasons
with use of unconventional
beds? Process technicians have.
They will considered harvesting
trends and make continuous
what was once thought to be
merely seasonal.
Accountants are calculating
net and gross profit margins.
Cranberry farming will be profitable.
Builders are here and with them, tools.
They constructed greenhouses
but also houses, maybe too now
they can produce cranberry beds.
But let's think outside the box,
of course not cranberry boxes,
which are built from exquisite white
pine & available for purchase. Salesmen
(but unfortunately no sales-women

as of now) have arrived and will
begin product demonstrations
to an only-moderately skeptical public.
The salesladies have arrived
and with them schedule-ladies,
and the big green schedule is for
the women, and the men's
schedule will be posted in a few
days. If you know of someone
interested in making the schedules,
we could always use more help.
The loggers have joined to clear
more farmland. Childcare workers
are now available to all working
moms and if mothers desire
to put their children above the needs
of the cranberry community, we will
strongly encourage them to limit
their with-children days but will
always allow them time, especially
during meals. Ad men are creating
some exceptional new ways of thinking
about the cranberry. Logistics are
of course a great concern, as we have
not found enough workers with that
experience yet, but we are creating
lessons-learned about that need
and have young boys and girls in
training to join soon. We would like

to thank an anonymous young man
who suggested blueberry infused
craisins at a point when blueberries
were overtaking our market shares.
Okay, it did not work as successfully
as one assumed, but the efforts
point to a strong sense of communal
well-being. The crop is expected
to be very large this year.
We will need all hands on dyke
creation in the east field as the soil
there is not as suitable as our other fields
A quick note to vandals who spray painted
the Southend processing facility:
you have shown a keen & artful
esthetic and if you come forward
you will be added to the marketing team
and no punishment will leveled against
you nor your family. In fact, we are all
a family here and we need to remember
that when considering future activities
that would be considered vandalous
by less developed cranberry farmers.

[Made tart by the weather]

"Cranberry Bogs, Large and Small FOR
SALE"

Made tart by the weather
and very much living. Able to
survive the cold in and be
made alive by water & food.
The most important element is air.

Winter Sandstorm

*In 1816, Captain Henry Hall of Dennis, Massachusetts discovered
that sand blowing on his cranberry vines stimulated the vine's growth.
(cranberries.org)*

A pang of cold arrives
and sand is storming.
The force blasts as
protection, a pang
of cold becomes
pain of winter. And yes,
the weather will be cruel
but, yes, the weather
brings a blanket with it too,
that is how it is. Life
spindles, and the sand, and
the sand and then the discovery!
I have kept myself. I have
been made in the weather,
You & I in winter. The storm.
I did not make the weather;
I stayed there, with you.

"Progress Report On the U.S. Department of Agriculture Cranberry-Breeding Project" Bain, Cran Berries 8(2): 4-5 (1943)[2]

In earlier reporting,
it was revealed
no one attempted
to improve varieties
by crossbreeding
prior to 1929.

This small bog
was generously
provided by the
Makepeace Company
to establish seedlings;
it is near Frogfoot bog.

These seedlings
may be seen at anytime
by anyone interested.
Please see both of
the previous years'
fruiting records.

2   Bain, Henry F. "Progress Report on the U. S. Department of Agriculture Cranberry-Breeding Project." Cran Berries 8, no. 2 (January 1, 1943): 4–5.

The sections were made
in the following manner:
each was first considered
independently from others.
Tables were created
for the individual plants

and the crosses were arranged
in descending order
of excellence
in yield, in freedom from rot,
in appearance (and when it
was possible) false bloom.

To even be considered,
a plant had to rank
near the top in one or
at least above middle
in the other
three classifications.
Plants with proper
qualifications were checked
for vine characters,
date of ripening, berry size
and if satisfactory they
were tentatively held until

the procedure was complete
for all crosses.

Further eliminations were then
made by balancing the best
plants against each other
as a group.

Note: in some cases,
no plants in a cross
rated high enough
to be kept.
These plants
were then removed.

Of the ones remaining
false blossom indices
were low,
as applied with the scale
of false bloom,
or they were eliminated.

The second test,
which included 40 seedlings,
was started in 1941.
It will naturally take
two years or more before
plots begin to fruit.

Parent names include:
Bennett, mother; McFarlin, father
Early black, mother; Aviator, father

Howes, mother; Searls, father
Shaw's Success & Paradise Meadow
McFarlin & Prolific

Henry F. Bain

You write on Cran Berries.
You mourn your son,
your namesake, Bain,
Staff Sergeant Bain,
awarded a Purple Heart
& an Air Metal. 5 others.
Born March 29, 1924
and just in time for war,
enlisted and died June, 1945.
His Service ID: 33750851.
The events of his life
and the event of his death.
"Killed in action".
Killed in the Philippines.
Entering the service
through Washington D.C.
Remembered by the people
of Wisconsin.

Hayden Separator MFG. CO.

And after the war...
foresee an even greater
future for the cranberry
industry. Plan *for that*
glorious day. We will repair
& serve you & *your*
cranberry equipment.
And until the war is over
we will continue to repair,
we will manufacture *a few*
Small Parts & remind you
Victory Will Come Some Day.

Strewnberry (Herbaceous Perennial)

		yes, it is useful. I.
There must have been rain-sprouts,
must have been limbs, possibly
a name. Maybe there is no name.
Maybe a name for everything I am
not. Straw strewn. Grown for this.

Stages Leading to Bloom

1. Tightbud
2. Bud swell
3. Cabbagehead
4. Bud break
5. Bud elongation
6. Roughneck
7. Hook
8. Bloom

See Beth Ann A. Workmaster, Jiwan P. Palta, and Teryl R. Roper's table in "Terminology for Cranberry Bud Development and Growth"

Highbush

I thought I was wild,
But all my life, I have
been farmed. Grown
with care, in a bed built
for me. I was watered.
I have been an effort
of difficult work regarding
how to raise fruit.
With cold-avoidance
strategies handed down
by farmers' practices
to survive the perpetual
possibility of frost.
I am the bitter product
of loving hands. Farmed,
clipped, and nourished.
Of course, there was harvest.
Of course, I was made useful.

Earnestly Praying for the Blessings of Heaven

Bless you. Bless this day.
                              May you enter into the day
& may it too be blessed. I believe   we are both alive.

Roughneck

The new stem elongates significantly, making all the flower bracts and buds visible. Flower stalks have not elongated. —Beth Ann A. Workmaster, Jiwan P. Palta, and Teryl R. Roper's *Terminology for Cranberry Bud Development and Growth*

In this stage, enter
as weather, pleasing &
rough like the season.

What is it to be seen
& not ready.
Stay busy being.

I can hear the weather.
The warnings of early May.
The flooded blooms:
weathered, alive.

For A Second Date

It got cold.
& I did not
want it the way
it was, so I put it
in a field.
How long
until I ruin this?
I want to be
a toaster-oven
user but really
I am watching
alfredo bubbling
in a saucepan
and thinking *why*
is he doing this?
May I take you
for take out then
sit at a Jiffy Lube?
Please stay with me
like a crabapple
in a tooth.
I want to shiver
with you.

Fireworm Versus Fruitworm

Because of the marshlands, fireworms
and because of unusually heavy snow,
fruitworms: *active during calm evenings
from June through early August,*
abundant because of snow adaptability,
preventable through control methods
using patented sprays during the *50%
out of bloom stage.* Be wary of worms.
Both are expected again this year.

You Can Not Say Bog Here[3]

It is inaccurate.
Growers in Wisconsin
refer to the beds built
for cranberries as
marshes. Technically
it is not a natural marsh
but if you are no longer
coastal, if you are in the
middle of this country,
and go out to a farm,
you learn to call it
the name the farmers
have established.

3   Title comes from personal communication with Dr. Workmaster

CFR[4]

bitter rot, cottonball
early, berry speckle
blotch rot, end, ripe
viscid, yellow, black.

One *overwinters in*
       plant debris

Two *persists in*
       living leaves

Three spores *dispersed*
       through floodwater

4   Cranberry Fruit Rot

Two Strategies for Freezing-stress Survival

The first is avoidance
but I do not avoid you.
No, mechanism, I pull
you into me, & tolerate.
I tolerate you. You are
so cold and I make it
useful to me. You are
so cold and I carry you
way up the stem of me.

When I Say I Love Him

He liked the clouds loud and crowding blue out
of sky.

> I want to remember only the food,

the chewing sounds.

His name hurts.

> Damn my haphazard practice!

Damn the nights
I practiced being abandoned then wasn't prepared.

When I say I love him,
I don't know what it meant or even what it means.

lowbush

I had saved that one for you,
that first handful of the year.
You thought, because you had
seen the name, tasted grocery
store domesticated versions
and canned-up holiday goop
that it would be bitter. I put them
into your hand. The amount
began to look much smaller there
but you cupped it and brought it to
your lips. This is the way I wanted
you to find out. This was my
marking of that whole year.
It was tart. It was sweet. It was
northern. I think you hated it
but you pulled me in for a kiss.

What Is Left

My father reminds me of the geese
how they enjoyed cranberry leaves
and the shade from the highbush in the hot,
carefully numbered days of summer.
My mother reminds me of *the ads, you know*
cranberries floating. She is always thinking
about water. Her body cuts through it.
When she found the river, she swam it, &
in a government pool, she moved through it
with more grace than I was accustomed to
seeing in that facility. When she got out, we
went to the water fountain and drank,
filled our bottles up, and drove back
to the river and drove over frozen deltas.
We were then home. My father reminds me
of the waddling geese, the way his body goes,
the way he drags his body through the day.
It is labor to walk, it is labor just to cut through air,
and he convinces himself, making one more
step. The mower pulls his body along the grass
and he steps slowly behind it. Unable to give
up his uses, unable to give away what
he has left of his legs. Every step is conscious.
My mother reminds me of *the cranberries,*
I don't think you understand, they were floating,
there's something there, something about

the water maybe. I hurry her off the phone.
Of course, there's something about the water,
the cranberries buoyed in their bath. My father,
like a goose, sits there in the cranberry water.
He can move, on the top of it, & he's paddling.

"America's farmers are not what some
people think."

All his life, he tractored
through cranberry bogs
until a neighbor passed.
He lifted into another's
tractor to help the other
family with their crops
of soy. Even though
most of it is only
destined for animals.

the discharges only occur when
homosexuals come to the official attention
of the *** *****

40

       for M
Tonight the lights of the television;
tomorrow, the sun and the next
day, maybe, more. Or maybe
we will one day tell.

Considering The Honorable

If you say it is winter, it is winter.
When in winter, I am astonished.
I stumble over *The Honorable*,
I say it. I say it over. Each time
the sounds loosen their meaning:
their repetition, the drip drip,
the drooped bloom of word
unreplenished, unable to hold –
in the cold – a quiet-sung dirge,
shivered phrases, an almost emptied
structure. Syllable, sound, syllable
garbled cadence of the pre-name,
marched out of lips, mowed vowel
stems stomped methodically down
into the permafrost word of what
our fathers were once called. Then
this *the* preceding even descriptor,
an indication of specificity before
the syllabic yawn. If there were
a word for breath in the clear cold
of winter. And there is! I utter it and
breathe a frail breath into bitter air.

Winter Solstice Eve

It is winter and we are
the beginning of what
we will be. Tomorrow
the sun will be tilted
the farthest from us,
tonight you are not here.
I have been so careful
because you are fruit.
No, you are also fruit
and have felt bruise.
I want to tell you
I know it is winter.

Left of Bloom

Nothing is the same here.
Not the seasons. I lived in
this one for so little time
the leaves here cling
so tight to their branches
and wave to a forgiving sky.
Not the grass, trampled
but still living where it is
found. Nor even the way
the birds are comfortable.
I remember when I fled
into the temperate
weather and was afraid
of how it touched me, soft.
Even the clouds are
merciful. Is that what
I wanted when I went
where I was pushed?
I want the world to be ruthless
with me. I want the air to
catch me quick in the lungs.
A living thing does not
consider

Winter Solstice

To me, it is a cold winter walk.
I have forgotten to name
the day the way you know it.
Ice is winking back the sun's
stare and staying crystaled
even in the noon. I stoop
to tie my shoe, an excuse
to see the world of ordinary dirt.
In all my other winters, I have
known snow, the blanket. I have
never held mud with my gloves
and taken off my hat in the heat.
And this is what I wanted to show
you. Someday it will be anything else
but for now, detail on a decaying leaf.

New Years

The Christmas trees are now mulch;
their wooden smell fermented in sun
and lingering over the heap of wood
chips. And that is how I remember it.
You were with me that night, the TV
was two minutes behind and all your
friends were loud & drinking, happy,
mostly, watching the times disagree
briefly. And that is how I remember
it. I did not bring a gift, nor champagne.
We kissed in your car before arriving.
I wanted to be yours for the last bits
of that horrible year. I wanted the fruit
taste of Truly. Cranberry Vodkas with
no extra sugar entered our discussion.
And that is how I remember it, I do not
have the name for it, but everyone else
seems to know what it is.

January 6, 2021

"The bog vined over and he watched it beginning to come into maturity" - *Clarence J Hall (Cranberries Magazine)*

James Madison left bogs of Virginia
to seek formal education in Princeton,
and attributed the move to his health,
or at least I think I heard that in *First
Principles* as I walked in Alexandria,
Virginia and listened to James Lurie's
voicing of the audiobook. It is all very
mundane. It is suddenly a nation.
I am walking where George Washing-
TON! walked before me! The street
lights are giving into the sun's strength
and the mandatory, enforced curfew
kept me from a walk until it lifted
at 6a.m. I keep turning off the audio
to think about America (a concept).
If you are very lucky, you never know
until it turns. Was I always American?
Only literally. Although I did not even
know it for years. I was in and not of
this world and applied this to the nation,
perhaps misguidedly. Then Whitman
introduced me, and I was an American.
It is the 7th of January, & I believe in

America: so young, a bit confused,
like me, even misguided. A stabilized
experiment is strengthened by testing.
There are an estimated 6,800 people
who died during the war, the first war.
Google gave me this in 0.37 seconds.
I do not know enough about the U.S.
but have seen the embarrassing proofs
of youths in a youthful nation making,
for themselves, a better place to live.
It is a dream in that it is something
I have not thoughtfully considered
or dared to make true to myself, yet.
I am walking in Alexandria, named
after a Scotsman who owned most
of the land. When I learned about
Alexander the Great, in high school,
I vowed to live in a city of his name.
Madison returned to Virginia, his
home, and I wish I could show him
this place I am living in now. Now
I am here, I am living & walking.
And I have never seen a bog here.
I am eight miles from yesterday's
events. And I am eight miles from
my apartment. I have looped too
far and am making my way back.

2 X 2 X 2

Two days is an injury. Two weeks is survival.
The study lasted two years.

Recipe with Note On Sugar Addition &
Secret Ingredient

For things like this
you boil out the bitter,
you resist the urge
to add sugar in,
and instead you turn
to all the other fruits.
Red wine is an option
but it should be fruity.
You may use other sweet
juices. Consider apple
or pear to surprise,
orange if you are ordinary
will work well also.
I find birch syrup to
be the most profound
addition because it
has more sweetness
than it has flavor.
It is my cooking secret,
revealed here
for the first time.
Some would use maple
syrup but then the flavor
is distinguishable.
One should always

surprise. One should
always turn to other
options: granulated sugar
not being one of them!

Bible Family

(as/an Autobiography)

We started… from scratch in 1992.
The way growers harvest is they flood
the beds, they take a machine
called the harrow… that knocks
the berries off.

"You see what you've done for the last
364 days of the year: protecting
these things through the winter,
taking care of them" Bible said,
gesturing to the marsh behind him.

"Then when I'm on the machine,
knocking… off… all the fruit…
I really enjoy that."

dream of living in California

I used to dream of living
on dust and chicken meat.
I played driftwood games
until the river rose, taking
them to some farther bank,
some out-of-reach beach,
having much less ordinary
grey sand, maybe a place
with no clay. A real shore.
I used to dream of living
off occasional gulps of sea,
where the water had weeds.
Not the glacier-fed river
meeting muddied delta
streams but the brine of an
entire ocean swishing
to sustain me. My throat
was hot when I thought
of California and I wanted
to sip it all. I wanted it to be
the place where I grew up
on my grandmother's farm
and also on the beach, also
in cities – all, all, all of them.
Pismo Beach was a place
& not just the sweatshirt's

cursive scrawled on my chest.
I did not stutter in California.
I wanted oranges on trees,
instead of boxed in pound
amounts, carried down-river
after trips into the city.
I thought of California
and I wanted to chew it up.
I wanted mouthfuls of city
life and sidewalks and streets!
My lisp was song in California.
It was never crowded or cold.
I was fit if I was in California.
California kept me warm.
I dreamt I could be anything.
Californian. Me.

I Have Never Been to New York

I am embarrassed by quiet nights,
water whirring in valves in the ceiling.
The floor, cold and carpeted and, yes, still cold.

The shutting of a door was more reliable
than a voice and I could tell a person by
the footsteps, their turning of the handle,

swoosh of the door. My father's lime syrup
sat unrefrigerated in his bottom right drawer.
The tonic and the gin, comfortably closeted.

We sliced our own cheese. I carried it
in plastic tubs, sealed in gallon bags, to all
houses. But in the *real*-world cheese was orange!

I wished our cows' milk tasted as artificial
as the bottles. In the morning, I milked the cows
and at 04:45, loaded their milk into a small tractor.

The long way back was once quiet
then there was a truck with an illicit radio.
Then the new barn truck got louder speakers.

Unloading the milk into the pasteurizer,
I would talk to the breakfast ladies,

one loading bread into the conveyor toaster

for 200 people, *no more Floors* another would
say as I washed out the five-gallon buckets,
turned them over to dry in the cheese room,

& loaded the truck with whey for the pigs.
Sometimes the lid was not tight and rancid
yellow whey would splash onto my jeans.

Sometimes the schedule would read *pigs*
and I would shovel manure, feed them,
and put out some straw. They were easy

to clean up for and friendly.
Sometimes the schedule said *slaughter*
no specificity — but I knew.

Sometimes it was messy; sometimes quick.
Sometimes I would wish I was in Chelsea
with purposeful red brick and seven or eight

stairs leading into an expensive apartment,
with bottled milk in the refrigerator!
I used to wish I didn't know

where milk came from.
I wanted to be a vegetarian. To listen
to the city's sounds as I walked home.

The only ambulance I heard was in a Madonna
song as I walked the ice bridge to the trading
post, cleaned for pop caps, and hoped for song codes

hidden under each lid. I knew they drank Coke
Zero in New York City. Fizzy. Glamorous
like ambulances singing to a busy night, like lights,

like the quiet of a bar where you ordered a whiskey
and sipped it slow in the only quiet you could find.
A polebarn was my bar. I drank beer and whiskey.

It was exactly New York, I could taste it in my throat.

harvesters used for wet harvesting are
colloquially called "beaters"

"To be a cranberry farmer you have to wear a lot of different hats."
—Cranberry Foreman Alex Manchester

Why do you want beautiful?
Without the farmer, or water.
The sky is blue not everyday.
Why is this ordinary? Breath.
This is not Los Angeles. Not
anywhere you have been before.
Not New York. But busy with
structure. Not a page, although
yes, I want to live forever.
I watched his veins. He carried
water buckets and I thought
I want to be

American invites you to enjoy a new and wonderful experience[5]

The year American announces
a non-stop four & half hour flight,
coast-to-coast! It is non-stop. *Now
for the first time, getting there
becomes a real pleasure.* And
"No Cranberries for President"
reports the Associated Press
within Annals of Technology
from the New York Times.
The President eats applesauce?
This sliced piece of cran-sauce
is about as American as massacre
and the color sticks to the inside
of its washed can. No one thinks
they want it, but it is still there.

5   Title takes its name from an American Airlines ad, Jan 1959

A Prayer to First Lieutenant Martin Everett Kranick

Let me be a *scene of many experiments*
where the *most active worker* believes I may
bring prosperity. Let me be a farm cultivated
during war. I have enlisted myself for America
and I believe in her, and I believe in them, in us.
Keep me in my belief as you kept your enlisted
oath made in April of 1942 in Omaha, Nebraska.
Accept me like your commission in June of 1943.
Navigate. Guide me. Show me where, how to go.
I will be brutal with the ones I love. I will not have
unchecked ruthlessness. Keep me competing.
Make me a wartime game; play me exceptionally!

"An Idea For Post-War"

a get-together of growers
may be a perfect way for
cranberry minded people

to meet. Perhaps in a central
place like Wisconsin.
And bring both coasts together

to *build unity among*
the cranberry industry
from various growing states.

Does the idea appeal to you?

A Note On Process Versus Perishability

Keep in mind, *cranberries are seasonable,*
more seasonable than perishable, and this
is equally true after they have been processed.
The process *reduces the perishability*
to a greater extent *than it lengthens the season.*
This, however, should and doubtless will change
with the continued promotion and *sale of processed*
cranberries.

Judgments of divorce/annulment filed in February 2019 at the Jefferson County clerk's office

Watertown, NY

I didn't think we would make it to not making it.
That public record would mention us together,
only in that we shared a line, a bullet, a last time.
Yes, the Sanfords, maybe the Cowing/Millans.
I could see someone with the name of Richardson
wandering just a bit. But your happy *J*,
I was surprised. Your jubilant scribble freed you.
I wanted to be unhappy with you, forever, wanted
my back to ache from sleeping on the floor
of your guest room, in a third floor apartment made
for geo-bachelors in the Army. I wanted to be
hungry every single night, to wake up to weekend
wine, or to you dressing for physical fitness with
your speaker pulsing electronic music that if I knew
the name of, you would never play again. Of course
I shazamed! I made an entire playlist of your songs
and I thought if I listened to them long enough…
it never worked.
I was jealous of your dog. I craved your attention
because it was possible and it was work. Hard
work. Like everything is. And I loved to exhaust
myself. I guess I thought Wilder would. Hawkinses,

true. And I have never been a fan of a Nelson, so.
The way you tied your laces made me never want
to have shoes. I was Old Navy and you wanted Gap.
The Rutiglianos ruptured. James and Fofana kinda
parted. Holland and Garnsey, contractually released.
I smiled when I thought of how happy your choppy
writing showed me you were. Curves always gave it
away. Like that love letter you wrote, you rambled,
you couldn't wait to send it so you called me too.
It was a same excitement. You knowing something
better and being eager to have every next minute of it.
The Collingtons called it off, Kehoes went from
I-dos to don'ts. Hotis, Reiger, Abbate, Hyde, Brewer.
I thought you wanted me how I wanted me, busy
Babcock, Burnham, Johnson & Johnson, Dominguez
I like what the city did, we could just sit for coffee.
Jackson, Robertson, Handson, Kearney, Allen & Paul
here is something to remember me by but I wanted
to have you. To laugh at other peoples' anniversaries
because ours was sometime in March, but we didn't
need to know when. The Audus bid adieu. Knowles
untied the knot, Edwards, Fahl & Bowling.
Sometimes, I thought *enjoy this.* Sometimes,
I wanted to be ordinary enough for us to be.
There were Penningtons. And Goodsells.
I don't remember washing our rice pan,
but the living room had three candles
or was it two?

Vibrates

The theory involves something vibrating
ignoring the tease of whatever-it-now-
-means, and it involves wine avoidance
strategies and do-not-order-those-burgers
methods passed down from a man who
watched me sweat, and did not even once
look away. When you are hungry, reach for
an apple, a glass of water, an apple, water.
The theory involves even more water, lots
and lots of water. A glass should always be;
full, the thing I loved about the fields
as you described them when I moved away.
When you said, what do you miss, it was
them. It was how mowing never seemed
to deplete them. How the sparrows always
buried their nests and so foolishly hoped,
like we were taught to hope, that somehow
the bailer would not come. The theory
was that a glass, a sip, should not be needed
but the needing was so necessary to me.
I have never been lonely in a field.
I don't think I have been thirsty in a field.
All of the theories of sitting in cold grass
didn't teach me how to be here. Vibrating
says the clothes are done. Vibrating says
a friend has called. Vibrating asks why

are you still drinking cheap wine? Can you
quit? Can you call sometimes? Call me
later. I won't. My feet ache on this pavement.
Every time I try to walk on the small patches
of grass, they disappear into brick, more brick.
The first time I heard crickets, it all sounded
artificial. Sprinklers rose from the ground
and sprayed the chirpings. More noise.
I remember irrigating the fields by the garden,
the labor always equaled the result. The closest
thing to crickets, where I'm from, is a bird chirp
quick, singular, more prayer than psalm.
Once they've found each other, in a crabapple tree
they sing and they sing, and it vibrates the ground.

Our Experiment Lasted Two Years

It was enough. And I miss it.
You gave me counted hours.
Gave data. I was information
thirsty and you were alive
and I had never lived before.
You wanted real silverware.
I wanted to learn everything
in the entire world for you.
I was the kind of eager that
only sat on half of the chair.
In a photo, I leaned into you.
On a walk, we drank small
champagne bottles. Cheers
to the photo of your dog.
The one that slept between
us and growled when I got
into bed. I was bad in bed
because I did not want to be
bad. I did not want to ruin it,
I guess I ruined it, didn't I?
You were a regime. I loved it.
You assembled the couch.
You took stairs one at a time.
Your mother thanked me
for loving you, that was all
she ever said to me. To you,

I was an omelet maker, taker
of earbuds, your dog walker.
We were something I wanted.
I was never strange to you.
I was part of the experiment
and you were the other part.

I Want To Be Useful

       Berry hung from branch
very eager to be very ripe.
Yes, I wanted to be blueberry
infused when I was another,
that other berry. I wanted to be
sold in stores, and chewed.
       A bitter, barely tasted,
brisk-weather loving berry.
Better-when-boiled-down
berry. You want to eat me
from a can now, don't you?
Burrowed in the snow berry,
found by its bright colors
and in ordinary bogs, berry.
Buried in its fruit form to be
another living thing making
bellies full in winter berry.
Round, held in your hands,
nestled next to others, found
among, found rarely by itself.
Nourished. And nourishing
when taken off of the vine.
Can be frozen, dried, packed,
saved for later, or for now.

Notes

The poems "Greenhouse" & "cran" were published in the *Midwest Review,* volume 9.

The poem "Stages Leading To Bloom" is a found poem. The original terminology was published by Workmaster, B.A., J.P. Palta, and T.R. Roper. 1997. Terminology for Cranberry Bud Development and Growth. *Cranberries Magazine.* (Feb): 11-14

The poem "Winter Sandstorm" was published in *Military Experience & the Arts,* volume 17

The poem "Vibrates" was published in *Guesthouse.*

The poem "Bible Family" takes all lines from "An inside look at cranberry growing" by McKenna Alexander, WQOW https://wqow.com/2020/10/28/an-inside-look-at-cranberry-growing/

The collected, archived *Cranberries: the national cranberry magazine* was hugely influential to this project. Many poems take lines, phrases, or ideas from it.

The scholarship of Dr. Workmaster has been another important part of this project. Many of her articles were influential in the crafting of this book but none more so than "Understanding Cranberry Frost" which is how this project began.

The poem "Earnestly Praying for the Blessing of Heaven" takes its title from personal communication with my brother Evan Eads.

The poem "dream of living in California" is an amalgamation of the first line and title of Rafael Campo's "California".

The poem "You Can Not Say Bog Here" take its title from personal communication with the poet and scholar Beth Ann Workmaster.

The poem "CFR" takes its title from a disease called "Cranberry Fruit Rot".

The poem "America's farmers are not what some people think." takes its title from a cranberry farmer's Facebook video.

The poem "Judgments of divorce/annulment filed in February 2019 at the Jefferson County clerk's office" takes its title from a news article by the same name.

The poem "I Want To Be Useful," along with the rest of the collection, celebrates Ocean Spray's Craisins & Craisins (Blueberry infused).

Notes on Thanks

Thank you, Jesus!

Thanks to Walnut the Crane.

I know I won't be able to thank everyone who made this book possible but I am ever grateful to all involved.

Thank you, Kirsten (Kai) Ihns, for more than I will ever be able to express here. I am grateful to have you in my life. Your edits! Your poems! Rapture!

Thank you to Dr. Beth Ann Workmaster – both as a poet and a scholar, you inspire me.

Thank you to the dead, especially: Derick and Lucie.

Derick Burleson. For the kisses. For the possibility of queerness that dragged me into your class. For the Miłosz poem that made me stay. For showing me, I was called for this. For ripping up a draft of my work and demanding excellence I did not know I was capable of. For withholding your recommendations unless I applied to the Iowa Writers' Workshop. For *Never Night*.

Lucie Brock-Broido. For the acceptance call. For teaching me how to negotiate in this terrifying world. For reminding me to be a flea. For telling me to go where I did not want to go. For *Stay, Illusion*.

Thank you, Kate Pendleton. You made me write poetry at work. You make me consider the world in ways that are foreign to me. I admire you and I love you.

Thank you to the Poetry Conspiracy.

Thank you to the concept of Jill Osier and to Jill Osier. My thanks to the faculty of the English Department at the

University of Alaska. Thank you, Sean Hill. Thank you, Gerri Brightwell, Richard Carr, Chris Coffman, Daryl Farmer, Terry Reilly, Eileen Harney, Eric Heyne, and Sarah Stanley. I deeply thank Jennifer Tilbury and Cindy Hardy.

Ernestine Shaankaláxt Hayes thank you for the blurb and the mentorship; I look up to you.

Christopher Salerno, thank you for your kind blurb-words. Does *The Man Grave* have room for one more?

My thanks too, to the Creative Writing faculty at the Iowa Writers' Workshop at University of Iowa: James Galvin, Josh Bell, Brian Blanchfield, Suzanne Buffam, Mark Levine, Jane Mead, Robyn Schiff, Emily Wilson, and Elizabeth Willis.

My thanks also to the Performance Studies theory faculty at the University of Maryland including James Harding, Frank Hildy, Caitlin Marshall and Van Tran Nguyen.

Brian Blanchfield, I want to put your name on its own line. Thank you for believing in my work and continuing to push me.

Thank you to my colleagues past and present who I cannot possibly fully list but will attempt. Rebecca Lawhorne, Heather Ringo, H. Warren, Kori Hensell, Jaclyn Bergamino, Chelsey Zibell, Danny Dyer. Lindsey Barr, Atiya Dorsey, Jordan Ealey, Matré Grant, Mina Kawahara, Marissa Kennedy, Margaret (Maggie) Lapinski, Alex Miller, Kristopher Pourzal, Jared Strange, Melissa Sturges. How does this *perform*?

Thank you to my students, past and present.

My thanks to the IWW people: Jennifer Adrian, Rachel Arndt, Nicole Balin, Emily Brown, Connie Brothers, Ben Bush, Emmett Buckley, Jackson Burgess, Moira Casados Cassidy, Ruth Corkill, that Harvard guy, Christina DeVillier, A. Duplan, Kelly

Hoffer, Domenica Martinello, Tony Flesher, Michael Gregory, Strummer Hoffston, Jane Huffman, Kirsten Ihns (yes again), Celine Izsak, Erin Kelleher, Benjamin Krusling, Jake Montgomery, Grayson Morley, Alyssa Moore, Alex Moss, Patty Nash, Julianna Neely, Alyssa Perry, Tanner Pruitt, Ethan Plaue, Z. Polach, Brit Siler, Seth Stephanz, Lindsey Stern, Kristen Steenbeeke, Andrew Smyth, Katrina Turner, Ryan Tucker, Devon Walker-Figueroa, Alicia Wright, Stella Wong, C. Wyatt, Deb West, Jan Zenisek, and anyone else whose name I forget to mention here.

Thank you to the Mercatus Center and my fellow Elinor Ostrom Fellows: Alex Bacall, Diksha Bali, Martina Beretta, Véronique Ehamo, Vivian Jin, Chayce Kenny, Juno Kim, Helen Kosc, Carlos Noyola, Naomi Nubin-Sellers, Cornelia Nyadroh, Jair Peltier, and Murielle Sandra Tiako Djomatchoua. And the brilliant Nicole Melnyk. Scholars including Ginny Choi, Chris Coyne, Kristen Collins, Stefanie Haeffele, Arielle John, and Virgil Storr thank you for showing me the connections between the arts and economics.

Thank you, Miss Euphoria.

My thanks to Juan Davila & Kalli Rolfe for allowing the use of my dream cover, the image Fig. 300

I am grateful to Sven and Rebel Satori Press for believing in and publishing the "Work".

I am grateful to the named/unnamed cranberry farmers. I celebrate your tenacious care.

I am grateful to the people of Whitestone, Alaska. Tenacious care… and so much more!

I am grateful to my parents, Elaine and Emerson Eads. Thank you for choosing difficult paths.

Emerson, Evan, and Eric – three squeezes.

Kylie, Abbie, Adelle, and Reaghann – LY2M2T

I am thankful to the behind-the-scenes characters and backstage helpers that made this book a possibility and then a reality.

www.ingramcontent.com/pod-product-compliance
Lightning Source LLC
Chambersburg PA
CBHW031402060726

47590CB00007B/2907